CURRICULUM
.LINKS ages 5–7

Around
our School

Suzanne Kirk

Credits

Author
Suzanne Kirk

Editor
Clare Gallaher

Assistant Editor
Dulcie Booth

Series designer
Lynne Joesbury

Designer
Catherine Mason

Illustrations
Gaynor Berry

Photographs
© Scholastic Ltd

Cover photographs
Lynne Joesbury

Photographic symbols
Geography © Photodisc, Inc.
Art & design, RE © Stockbyte

Published by Scholastic Ltd,
Villiers House,
Clarendon Avenue,
Leamington Spa,
Warwickshire
CV32 5PR
Printed by Bell & Bain Ltd, Glasgow
Text © Suzanne Kirk
© 2003 Scholastic Ltd
1 2 3 4 5 6 7 8 9 0   3 4 5 6 7 8 9 0 1 2

Visit our website at www.scholastic.co.uk

British Library Cataloguing-in-Publication Data
A catalogue record for this book is available from
the British Library.

ISBN 0-439-98436-X

Contents

Introduction

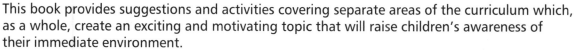

This book provides suggestions and activities covering separate areas of the curriculum which, as a whole, create an exciting and motivating topic that will raise children's awareness of their immediate environment.

Young children's experiences of their surroundings widen day by day. With every new experience their curiosity and interest is awakened. At first their world centres on the familiarity of family and home. School life introduces them to a broadening environment. They meet new people, make unusual journeys, pass strange buildings. During this stage children need to be encouraged to look around, to explore, to ask questions and make connections. As they travel to school, visit the shops, library or sports centre, they can be guided towards noticing what is around them. They remember new people, begin to recognise new places. In this way they will begin to understand how the locality directly affects their lives. A sense of belonging to the community will emerge. Through acquiring knowledge, skills and understanding of their world, confidence in themselves will increase.

Around our school is an essentially geography-based book which incorporates elements of RE and art and design. It will help you create an interesting and relevant topic to teach over a number of weeks which will enable children to explore the immediate surroundings of their school. The emphasis of this book is to develop the children's awareness of the local environment through a range of activities directly linked to their everyday experiences. Opportunities are provided for careful observations, exploration and discovery. Fieldwork is an important element of this topic, with children making expeditions into their locality.

What subject areas are covered?

This book covers the geography QCA Scheme of Work unit 1: 'Around our school – the local area'. This links naturally and successfully with the RE unit 1F: 'What can we learn from visiting a church?' and art and design unit 2C: 'Can buildings speak?'. Bringing these areas of the curriculum together creates an appropriate topic for Key Stage 1 children. The topic starts with the children observing from the playground and leads to excursions into the surrounding streets and open spaces.

Outdoor experiences are essential if children are to develop a complete picture of themselves within the community of their home and school. Several journeys each with a different focus would be ideal (see Fieldwork opportunities, page 9). A visit to a local church is invaluable so that children appreciate the importance to people of a place of worship, its relevance within the community and discover the significance of the building itself. The neighbourhood surrounding the school can provide inspiration and ideas for artwork. New skills can be practised, observations encouraged and creativity expressed.

Throughout the topic it is important to emphasise the positive features which surround the school so that the children think of it as a good place to be. Perhaps there is a good view, many trees close by, interesting places to walk, plenty of shops nearby, open spaces, places to play, a good system of transport, lots of different people to see and meet.

Involving parents and carers is a useful strategy and shared learning experiences between child and adult can play a valuable part in the success of this topic (see Involving parents, page 7). As children travel to school, move around the area or visit local amenities, adults can be encouraged to discuss, listen and point out interesting features and happenings.

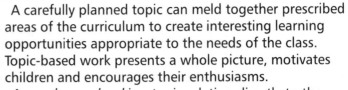

Introduction

Teaching specific subject areas through a topic

While it is important to distinguish the separate subject areas of geography, RE, and art and design, natural links can be difficult to ignore and are extremely useful in relating one area of work with another. One subject focus can provide an opportunity to explore another field.

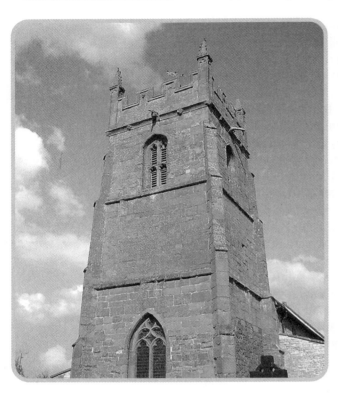

A carefully planned topic can meld together prescribed areas of the curriculum to create interesting learning opportunities appropriate to the needs of the class. Topic-based work presents a whole picture, motivates children and encourages their enthusiasms.

Around our school is a topic relating directly to the children's immediate experiences. It brings together the things they see each day, the sounds which are familiar to the neighbourhood, the surfaces they touch as they move about and the scents evocative of places they know.

A special focus on a local Christian church represents the RE element of the topic. The position of the church in the community, the building itself and its importance to the people are included.

Buildings in any environment provide a rich source of inspiration for work in art. In this topic, children have plenty of opportunity for observational drawings. They can use the patterns and shapes they see to develop their creative ideas and learn and practise new skills. The elements of art and design can be used to demonstrate the achievements of the topic, bringing it to a successful conclusion.

Getting started

Familiarise yourself with the area surrounding the school and find out where the further reaches of the catchment area are. Pinpoint the 'centre' of the community should the school be away from that area. Try to imagine how the children feel when walking along the surrounding streets. What will they see and hear? How will they feel? What will be important to them?

Take a close look at any outstanding buildings or features in the locality and note those relevant to everyday life such as any shops, the library, town hall, bank, public houses and eating places, parks and open spaces, the leisure centre. Make special arrangements to visit a local Christian church when preparing for section 4.

Look out for useful places to visit and find the best route along which to take the children as they explore their neighbourhood. Locate safe places to cross roads and find suitable key points along the route where children can safely gather to listen, ask questions and observe. Talk to people from the local church, the staff of the library, those who work at the town hall, in local shops, and so on.

Take photographs or a video film which will be valuable as a reference when planning as well as useful when highlighting specific aspects of the neighbourhood with the children. Begin a collection of material relevant to the surrounding area including photographs, postcards, booklets and so on. (See Resources below for a detailed list.)

Involving parents

Parental involvement is vital if children are to get the most from this topic of work. Adults can encourage children as they are out and about in the neighbourhood. As the interest grows, children will enjoy sharing information and experiences with their parents.

Prepare a letter to parents and carers outlining the topic and explaining how they can encourage their children to understand more about their neighbourhood. Explain that this can be done in a light-hearted manner through fun activities and normal conversation. Ask parents to point out interesting things as they travel around with their children – buildings such as the library, bakery, post office and factory. They should talk about the roads they use, where they lead to and how to stay safe where there is traffic. Remind them about pointing out distant landmarks, such as a tall chimney, hillside or line of trees. Suggest they invent simple games with their children which encourage observation or help with remembering. Special instructions will be helpful to parents when the children are involved in the activities of section 2 (see page 20).

Section 2 involves children discovering things for themselves away from the classroom, when help from parents and carers is essential. Adults need to be fully informed of what is involved and exactly when they are required to help. In good time, perhaps at the beginning of the half term in which the work 'Around our school' will take place, send a letter out to inform parents/carers. Explain that the children will be spending several weeks investigating their neighbourhood starting with activities within the school grounds. Then they will move on to looking at the outside of their houses and the routes they take to get home from school, when they will need the guidance and encouragement of parents and carers.

The children's enthusiasm will also help to keep parents informed and involved throughout this topic of work. Promise that the parents will see the final efforts of the class either as a display, exhibition or celebratory event as a climax to this area of work.

Resources

Photographs taken in and around the neighbourhood are an invaluable resource for this topic of work. Although it is always useful to take photographs when the children are on visits and involved in fieldwork, a bank of photographs taken before the activities begin will provide an extra dimension and an important reference for this work. Photographs can be

Getting started

used where a visit or excursion is not possible and for reminding the children of situations and events in their local environment. They are extremely important for adding value and interest to displays.

Walk around the neighbourhood with a list of the features, buildings and people you wish to photograph. Alternatively, enlist a parent or carer who enjoys photography to help out, providing them with a detailed list of the subjects for pictures. The following photographs would be useful:

Section 1 – patterns and shapes as seen from the school grounds; the church from the school grounds (if this is appropriate)

Section 2 – a selection of local street name signs

Section 3 – landmark buildings and other features such as postbox, signpost, traffic island and so on

Section 4 – photographs of exterior features of the church; special features and Christian artefacts within the church

Section 5 – people in the streets involved in everyday activities; attractive and less attractive parts of the neighbourhood; busy and quiet areas; examples of changes occurring

Section 6 – people doing jobs (indoor and outdoor examples); local play areas, perhaps with children occupied in different activities; leisure opportunities.

Further details are given in the preparation section of each activity.

Maps are frequently used in this topic of work. Large-scale maps are essential when extending children's awareness of their immediate locality. It might be appropriate to make several large copies of a simplified version of the area which will be studied; this will eliminate unwanted information a printed map might give and avoid confusion. (Ensure that you keep within the guidelines of your LEA licence with Ordnance Survey.) Decide on the extent of the map to be drawn, which might be the village, neighbourhood or centre of a town. Draw only a basic outline of familiar streets; other features can be added as part of each activity.

Other resources: try to collect as many of the following as possible:

■ material specific to the area surrounding the school – pictures, postcards, photographs, newspaper cuttings, leaflets, local maps, books, town trails, country walks and so on; information about specific buildings, streets and open spaces (the local studies department of the library will often have useful information)

■ photocopies of pictures of buildings and features relevant to the activities, which can be included with the children's individual collection of work, for example a representation of the church, a photograph of a local landmark and a street scene

■ pictures showing a range of buildings, particularly different types of houses; street scenes, traffic, people engaged in everyday activities; parks, open spaces and countryside

■ aerial photographs of the local area as well as any others from which children can identify famous landmarks

■ video material of different types of buildings including churches, street scenes showing traffic and general activity; also locally made film showing special events, church services, familiar street scenes and so on (these can be edited to show features and events relevant to the activities described, such as familiar buildings and important landmarks)

■ information relating to the local Christian church, booklets, postcards and so on; Christian artefacts such as a cross emblem, a bible and hymn book; pictures and photographs of different types of churches

■ camera for taking photographs prior to the activities when necessary, for using during visits and so on

■ directional indicators; compass points painted permanently on the playground are useful as the children get to know in which direction north, south, east and west are; portable directional indicators such as circles of card with the four points marked are helpful but need to be orientated for the children each time they are used

■ for fieldwork – clipboards, chalk, string, pencils, paper worksheets as appropriate, basic first aid kit

■ art materials – paints and painting equipment, pastels, crayons (some suitable for making rubbings), card, large sheets of paper, clay or papier mâché, tools for working with clay

■ photocopiable pages, which can be adapted as appropriate.

Fieldwork opportunities

The activities which comprise *Around our school* provide valuable opportunities for children to experience working outdoors in the locality. For the topic to be successful, at least one excursion around the neighbourhood and a visit to a local Christian church are essential components of this area of work.

Through the activities in this book, children are encouraged to explore their neighbourhood, carefully observing as well as becoming aware of the sounds and scents around them. They are encouraged to ask questions, form opinions and make decisions. Fieldwork should be enjoyable. Children are understandably excited about leaving the classroom but should understand that fieldwork is school work in a different environment where they can explore, observe and find out new things for themselves:
Section 1 – fieldwork from within the school grounds
Section 2 – research at home, then information brought back to school
Section 3 – a walk around the neighbourhood to identify buildings and features
Section 4 – a visit to a Christian place of worship
Section 5 – a walk around the neighbourhood to identify different types of places
Section 6 – a visit to a place of work.

Work outside the school grounds needs to be very carefully organised:

■ Enlist extra help from other adults so that children can be cared for in small groups.

■ Plan the excursion in detail. Brief all helpers thoroughly. Make sure they know the route to be taken and are clear about procedures for crossing roads. Explain where stops will be made and what the children are expected to do.

■ Make sure the children are well informed about the purpose of the excursion, what they are to look out for, any recording to be done and the behaviour expected of them. Talk about speaking quietly when out, being respectful to people they might meet, taking care especially in busy areas. Remind them about safety issues, particularly involving traffic. Insist they stay close to the adult leader of their group.

■ Carry with you a basic first aid kit, extra pencils and paper, and a mobile phone.

■ Suggest suitable clothing, ensuring the children have hats and gloves when it is cold and sun hats and rainwear as appropriate. Encourage the correct type of footwear for brisk walking.

■ Check LEA guidelines for out-of-school visits.

Introducing the topic to the children

Present the topic as an exciting prospect for both yourself and the children, something to look forward to with many interesting activities. Create a sense of discovery. Explain that there will be lots to find out about the places around school, that visits will be made and there will be people to meet. Also that children will need to keep their eyes open and each one of them can play an important part by looking around and noticing things. Explain that, as they live close by, they will know a lot of things already.

Point out that there will be opportunities to draw, paint and model using all kinds of interesting materials and that you hope they will help to create a splendid display by the end of the topic to show everyone what has been discovered about their neighbourhood. Consider how useful the information collected will be to newcomers as well as visiting friends and relatives.

Suggest the children introduce the theme of the topic to their parents and carers. Encourage the children to talk to adults and pass on the news about what will be involved. About this time inform parents by letter, explaining how they can help (see Involving parents, page 7).

Starting points

It might be useful to elicit the children's responses about their local area before starting the topic. With little prompting, find out how much they know about the surrounding area. Is it a town or in the countryside? Is it a quiet or busy place? What towns or villages are nearby? Do the children like living in this area? What are the best things about the neighbourhood? What are the things they do not like? Have they always lived here? Do their relatives live close by or far away? How do they travel when they go anywhere? Do they think they know everything about the area? What would they like to find out?

What can we see from our school?

FOCUS

GEOGRAPHY

GEOGRAPHY
- looking outwards from school to immediate surroundings
- school in relation to neighbourhood
- observational activities and fieldwork from school grounds
- orientation in relation to local environment

ART & DESIGN

ART AND DESIGN
- pattern and shape in the immediate environment

RE

RE
- identifying a nearby church

GEOGRAPHY

ACTIVITY 1

IDENTIFYING NEARBY FEATURES

Learning objective
To observe and identify nearby features which are characteristic of the local environment.

Resources
Chalk and string when outdoors; a directional indicator which can be marked on the ground near the area chosen for observing (or a small card directional indicator); photocopiable page 17; pencils and crayons for recording when indoors.

Preparation
Find the most suitable spot for observing the immediate environment from within the school grounds. Children need to see buildings, which can be close up, outlines or parts of buildings, and some features such as lamp-posts, fences, hedges, trees. Find out which way is north and mark the four compass points on the ground if possible. Otherwise, make a small directional indicator out of card which can be orientated when outside.

Activity

Take the children into the playground or other suitable area within the school grounds. Ask them to identify any features they can see which might be interesting such as buildings, rooftops, a lamp-post, trees, fields and open spaces. Allow the children to determine what is identified at this stage. Help them to relate their own position close to the school with the features identified. For example: *If I look this way, I mostly see houses. Over there we can see a road with traffic. I cannot see any trees when I look in this direction.* Encourage the children to use words and phrases such as *facing, behind, in front, over there, this way, direction.*

Ask the children to stand and face some of the chosen features as you draw chalk lines or stretch out string in the direction of each one, radiating from a central spot.

Tell the children to choose two or four things they can see to record when they return to the classroom. They might decide to choose something from two or four different directions.

(On another occasion, take the children out to listen for sounds of their neighbourhood and repeat the activity based on what they have heard. Talk about hearing but perhaps not being able to see some things.)

Recording

Photocopiable page 17 allows children to draw and write words or sentences describing the features they have recognised.

Differentiation

Children:
■ choose the two features which interest them the most, writing words to accompany their drawings
■ choose two features from opposite directions which they describe using sentences
■ choose features from four directions – north, south, east and west –using sentences to describe their choices.

Plenary

Select some children to show their work and talk about the reasons for their choice of features. Is there a feature that lots of children have chosen? Is there something only one person has chosen?

Talk about features which cannot be seen from the school, perhaps trees, lots of traffic or the sea. Point out that children at other schools might have these things in their view.

Display

Temporarily display the children's work for comment and discussion.

ART & DESIGN

ACTIVITY 2

LOOKING FOR PATTERNS AND SHAPES

Learning objective

To record from first-hand observation details of pattern and shape in the immediate environment.

Resources

Large and small sheets of drawing paper; clipboards; pencils and crayons with thick leads; pastels, paints and painting equipment; chalk; a camera; board or flip chart (if required).

1

Preparation

Decide upon one or more positions within the school grounds from where the children will be able to observe a variety of patterns and shapes. If it is more convenient, take photographs of particularly characteristic patterns and shapes beforehand.

Activity

Take the children outside and point out an example of a pattern or interesting shape, such as a line of buildings, a group of similar windows, a row of chimneys. Then ask the children to spot other examples. They might notice railings, pipework, paving, tiles, signs, or clouds, trees and outlines of hills. Use vocabulary such as *pattern, shape, square, rectangle, curve, straight, pointed, round, wavy*. Copy some of the patterns onto a large sheet of paper on the ground or perhaps draw directly on the playground. Take photographs of some particularly characteristic shapes.

Back in the classroom, talk about the patterns and shapes the children have noticed. Where did the children see a circle shape, a square, or a shape like a letter H in the environment? What made a pattern of triangles? What sort of patterns do windows make? Were there any wavy patterns? As you discuss, encourage the children to trace the shapes and patterns with their hands, particularly distinguishing between straight line and wavy patterns. Begin a pattern on the board or large sheet of paper and choose a child to continue it across the page. Demonstrate with other patterns and then encourage the children to create their own using crayons, pastels or paints.

Patterns and shapes

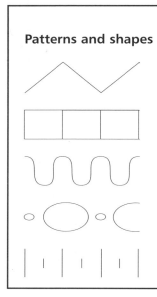

Differentiation

Children:
- use a starter sheet comprising the beginnings of patterns as a guide to drawing their patterns (see left)
- identify and record patterns they have remembered from their observations
- record a greater variety of patterns including straight and wavy line patterns, perhaps giving each pattern a descriptive title.

Plenary

Draw the children's attention to the artwork (see Display) and discuss which patterns represent the features they have seen outside. Distinguish between mathematical shapes which usually make regular patterns, and natural shapes which are more random.

Display

Create a frieze or border around the room using some of the patterns. Display any photographs taken or the patterns copied outside next to the children's work to show how the designs have evolved.

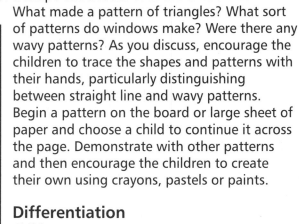

GEOGRAPHY

ACTIVITY 3

NEARBY AND FAR AWAY

Learning objective
To recognise that some features are nearby even though they perhaps cannot be seen, and that some are further away.

Resources
Card for making signpost pointers; postcard-sized pieces of card for sorting activity; paper for recording; pencils and crayons; photocopiable page 18.

Preparation
Make signpost pointers from pieces of card and write on each a name of a place or feature, some which are nearby and some which are further away. These can be held by the children or attached to an upright pole to represent a portable signpost.

Provide cards with sketches or symbols to represent nearby and distant features. Postcards of local places could be used and include the children's drawings as the activity proceeds. Make sure you know which way is north, perhaps drawing a directional indicator on the ground.

Activity
In the playground, ask the children to point out which features they can see that are close to the school. Then talk about the features that the children know are close by but cannot be seen because they hidden, or are perhaps smaller than things which are really close. Can the children guess the direction of things they cannot see – perhaps the main road, the post office, the motorway? Discuss the phrase *as the crow flies*. Ask the children to point in the direction the crow would need to fly to reach the church, the shops, the sports centre and so on. Choose some children to make themselves into a signpost by holding pointers made from card on which the names of relevant features have been written.

Move on to features which are further away. Ask the children to point out any distant things they can see, perhaps a faraway hill, trees on the horizon, a pylon, tall building or other landmark. If views are restricted, ask the children to tell you of places they know which are far away as well as others which are even further away. They might mention towns they visit, then London, Scotland, America and so on. Encourage the children to face the directions of the places they talk about and think of the crow flying to them. Make use of appropriate signpost pointers. Use a directional indicator to decide in which direction children can see the furthest.

Recording
Back in the classroom, ask the children to select one or perhaps two nearby features, which could be a lamp-post, bus shelter or tree, and one or two faraway features such as a distant building, motorway or sports field, to draw and write about. Use photocopiable page 18, as appropriate. Show the children the postcards and allow them to use the cards for inspiration if they need to.

Differentiation

Children:
- use photocopiable page 18 to record features nearby and far away, using headings as appropriate
- record nearby and faraway features, writing accompanying sentences
- record nearby and faraway features, using drawings and sentences and indicating the directions in which they were seen.

Plenary

Give the cards of nearby and distant features and places to some children to hold while others group them according to whether they are nearby or far away.

Display

Leave the cards on display so they are available for children to use in pairs inventing their own sorting games.

ACTIVITY 4

RE

IS THERE A CHURCH NEAR OUR SCHOOL?

Learning objective

To recognise a local church and begin to understand its importance in the community.

Resources

Photographs or drawings of the local church; if available, an aerial photograph showing the church and its position in relation to the school; clipboards; drawing paper; pencils.

Preparation

Collect and display drawings and pictures of the local church.

Activity

If any part of the church can be seen from the school grounds, use this as the starting point of the activity. How much can be seen will determine the focus of the initial discussion and later the recording. Find out if the children can identify the building and ask how they can tell it is a church.

If a church is not visible from the school, it might still be appropriate to go outside and look for it. Ask why the church cannot be seen. Perhaps it is too far away, hidden by taller buildings, or nearby but hidden by high walls which are close to the school and so restricting the view. Ask the children to point in the direction in which they think the church is. Which way would they start out to get there? Which direction would the crow fly to get there? Encourage some children to use a directional indicator to determine in which direction the church is.

Back in the classroom, show the children a drawing or photograph of the church and talk about it. Does the church have any special features such as a tower, spire or dome? What are the windows and roof like? How is it different from a house? Is it bigger, taller, made of different materials? Does it look old? Is it newly built? Which buildings are taller than the church?

Show the children an aerial photograph of the area. Help them to find the school and the church. Can they see any familiar features which identify these buildings such as the playground, the roof of the school; the spire of the church or the churchyard? Relate the position of the school to that of the church. Trace the crow's route. Perhaps try to find a walking route.

Recording
Encourage the children to make a drawing of the church – if appropriate, the view they have of the building from the school, otherwise using drawings or photographs.

Differentiation
Children:
■ make a simple drawing of the church and add an appropriate title
■ draw the church including important features and describing what they see in words or simple sentences
■ make a more detailed drawing of the church with a description of how to recognise the building.

Plenary
Admire the drawings made by the children and encourage them to point out the important features of a church building in each other's drawings.

Talk briefly about the importance of the church to people in the community – that it is a place to get together, to meet each other, a place to worship, a special building to admire.

Display
Use the photographs of the church together with the children's drawings to add to the display.

ACTIVITY 5

GEOGRAPHY

WHAT PASSES BY OUR SCHOOL?

Learning objective
To find out about the different types of people and traffic that pass the school.

Resources
Clipboards with paper on which to record the children's observations; photocopiable page 19; pencils and crayons.

Preparation
Decide on a suitable time and a convenient position within the school grounds from where the children can observe safely the passing traffic. Organise the children into groups or pairs with an adult or child in charge of the recording. Anticipate what traffic might pass, preparing a tally chart with simple drawings or symbols down one side of the page, but leaving space for anything unexpected to be included.

1

What can
we see
from our
school?

Activity

In the classroom, tell the children that they will be going out to see what passes by the school. Inform them whether they are working as a class, in groups or pairs. They should look out for anything that moves, which might be people, animals or vehicles. Explain how, to help them remember, a tally chart can be used, with a tick beside a symbol, picture or word representing each time something is seen.

When outside, allow about 10–15 minutes for observing. Remind the children to report their observations for recording on the tally chart so that nothing will be forgotten. Record such things as people walking, different vehicles, cyclists, dogs, horses and so on. Depending on the location of the school there might be tractors or boats passing by too, or planes flying overhead.

Back in the classroom, talk about the range of movement the children have seen. Perhaps there seemed to be more of one type of activity than any other, for example more people walking dogs than lorries passing, more cars than horses. Was there anything they did not expect? What was the most interesting thing which passed by? Talk about things which the children did not see. Perhaps no boats sailed past the school – why was this? Discuss where the people might be going – to work, to the shops, to a nearby town. Did anyone actually call in and visit the school?

Recording

Provide the children with photocopiable page 19 on which they can indicate which of the things passed by the school while they were observing and which they did not see. On the reverse of the page they can draw and write about the moving thing they found most interesting. If there was a reasonable range of movement with convenient numbers, it might be possible to convert the results into a graph.

Differentiation

Children:
■ use photocopiable page 19 to record simply *yes* or *no* as to which things passed by
■ use photocopiable page 19 and write a sentence to comment on the frequency of things which passed
■ make an ordered list of the frequency with which things passed the school, perhaps converting the results into a graph.

Plenary

Ask the children if they think many people and things pass the school each day or just a few. Would they describe the road as busy or quiet? Consider when the children themselves pass by instead of coming into school.

GEOGRAPHY

What I can see from our school

When I look one way I can see…

When I look another way I can see…

SCHOLASTIC

Nearby and far away

I saw these things near to our school.

_____

_____

I saw these things far away from our school.

What passed by our school?

person walking

car

lorry

dog with owner

cyclist

boat

SCHOLASTIC

Section 2

Where do I live?

FOCUS

GEOGRAPHY

GEOGRAPHY
■ the child's house as a building
■ position of the house in relation to the school
■ introduction to large-scale maps and plans
■ independent observation; collecting information
■ introduction to geographical terms including *map, route, address, graph, feature, aerial photograph, neighbourhood*

ART & DESIGN

ART
■ developing awareness of the textures of buildings through making rubbings

Preparation for section 2

In this section children will be expected to investigate and make discoveries away from the school with the help of parents or carers. It is important therefore that parents and carers are aware of what the children will be doing and are provided with details in a letter. Briefly outline each activity for this section where help is required and explain how the adults can guide and encourage the children (see 'Getting started', page 7). Tell the children what is happening from day to day, so that they feel confident to explain to their parents the necessary details:

■ 'This is my house'. In this activity the child's task is to observe features of their own house and make a drawing on the photocopiable sheet provided, ticking any of the features listed which they can see. Parents can help by finding a good safe position from where the child can observe and draw, asking questions which help to identify common and unusual features and encouraging the addition of extra features to the list which the child has observed.

■ 'Patterns from my house'. Children will have practised making a rubbing at school and will be able to explain to their parents how to proceed. Paper and crayon will be provided. Children feel the different textures of materials of their houses such as brick, wood, plastic, stone, metal, and choose one to make a rubbing. Parents can help by listening to their child's instructions on how the task is performed and by holding the paper.

■ 'My address'. Each child finds out about their address. Parents should help their child to look for the number on their house and locate the sign showing the name of the street where they live. They should encourage their child to remember their address orally, line by line.

■ 'Finding my way home'. Children observe the order of buildings and features on their journey home in preparation for drawing a map back at school. A page will be provided to assist with observations and the child can attempt a practice map on the reverse side of the paper. Parents can help by pointing out buildings such as the post office, library, factory and so on, and features such as corners, postboxes, places where the road is crossed. They should encourage their child to remember the order in which things are passed. For those children who travel a distance by car or bus, parents could concentrate on the first part of the journey home through the immediate neighbourhood, perhaps naming a specific spot where they might finish observing.

ACTIVITY 1

THIS IS MY HOUSE

GEOGRAPHY

Learning objective
To observe houses and identify their common features.

Resources
Pictures of different types of houses; photocopiable page 27; cards, board or flip chart, or large sheet of paper; pencils and crayons.

Preparation
Make sure parents and carers have been informed of what is involved in this activity. Decide how long to give the children before you expect their work to be returned. Write the names of the common features of houses on cards, the board or a large sheet of paper for the children to refer to when they label their drawings. Alternatively, the photocopiable page can be used as a reference for key vocabulary.

Activity
Explain to the children that you want them to look very carefully at the front of their house. Suggest they find a good but safe place to stand so they can have a long careful look at the building and then make a drawing. Stress that if it is necessary to leave the garden or house itself to get a better view (this is particularly relevant if the child lives in a flat), an adult they know must be with them.

When they look at the house, can they see a door? How many windows are there? Is there a chimney? What is the roof like? Is it a special shape? Does it have slates or tiles? What sort of a pattern do they make? Ask the children to remember what other features the house has – perhaps a gate, steps, path, a garage. Can they tell if the house is joined on to another building or can they walk all the way round it? Ask the children to look for the number of their house (in preparation for activity 3). Is it on the door, the wall or perhaps the gate? Does their house have a name?

Show the children the photocopiable page which you will provide for their drawing. Explain how they can use the large space for the drawing and then put ticks against the features in the list which they can see as well as adding any other features they see which are not mentioned. If appropriate, the children can be encouraged to write sentences on the reverse of the photocopiable page to describe their house. Make it clear to the children when you want their drawings to be returned.

When the children have returned the information they have collected about their house, discuss any problems encountered. Was it always easy to find a good spot for observations? Perhaps the view of the house was obscured by a large tree or other building. Ask if anyone discovered something they had not noticed before, perhaps a differently shaped window or a pattern in the brickwork. Was it difficult to see the roof and see what it was made of? Discuss the drawings and compare them with pictures of different types of houses on display. Ask if the children can see a house similar to their own, perhaps with the same number of windows or a door in the same position.

Recording
If appropriate, the children can add a heading or labels to their drawings, or write sentences to describe their observations, for example *The front of my house has one door and three windows. I could not see a chimney.*

Differentiation
Children:
- draw their house and identify the key features
- add extra details to their drawings, labelling the key features
- write sentences to describe the front of their house to accompany the drawing.

Plenary
As an example, select one child to answer questions about their house. Ask questions such as: what colour is your front door? How many windows are there on the front of your house? Does it have a chimney? Can you walk all the way round your house? Then, in pairs, children can ask each other similar questions and exchange information.

Display
Arrange pictures of a variety of houses which can be used to make comparisons with the children's drawings of their own houses.

ACTIVITY 2

PATTERNS FROM MY HOUSE

ART & DESIGN

Learning objective
To record from first-hand observation the textures of buildings.

Resources
Sheets of plain paper for making rubbings; small pieces of thick crayons.

Preparation
Decide when the children will practise their rubbings at school and how long you will give them to make their rubbings at home before returning them.

Activity
Take the children into the playground and identify different textures such as stone, brick, wood, plastic and metal. Give the children the opportunity to feel the materials while closing their eyes, and comment on their smoothness and so on. Then demonstrate how to make a successful rubbing. Explain that the paper must be held firmly so someone needs to help, and the crayon is rubbed from side to side and in that direction only.

Let the children make their own rubbings, working in pairs, choosing a texture and taking it in turns to hold the paper while their partner uses the crayon. Examine the completed rubbings. Is it always easy to tell what the material was? Are all the rubbings of wood similar in any way? Have any letters or patterns emerged (as on metal grates and so on)?

After the rubbing practice, give the children a piece of paper and a crayon and ask them to make a rubbing of part of the outside of their house. Suggest they choose a really interesting part, and ask them to remember what sort of material they have rubbed. Emphasise being safe, not climbing to reach a particular area, and asking a parent or carer's permission. Point out that someone will be needed to help by holding the paper while the rubbing is done.

When the rubbings are returned, talk about the children's efforts. Did they encounter any problems? Perhaps it was windy or the best things were out of reach. Compare them with the rubbings done in school. If appropriate, ask the children to write a simple caption or explanation to be displayed with their rubbing.

Differentiation
Children:
■ give their rubbing a title and provide an oral explanation about the activity
■ write an explanatory label to accompany their rubbing
■ provide sentences to explain what their rubbing shows.

Plenary
See if the children can easily identify any of the textures from the rubbings and sort them according to the materials.

Display
Use some of the rubbings as a background or border to display work carried out during the activities in this section.

ACTIVITY 3

MY ADDRESS

GEOGRAPHY

Learning objective
To recognise an address and understand its significance.

Resources
Photographs of local street name signs; large-scale map of the area; photocopiable page 28; pencils.

Preparation
Collect envelopes addressed to the school; write each child's name and address on a blank envelope; take photographs of street names and perhaps rubbings if any signs are in relief and easily accessible. A few days before the activity ask the children to look out for the name of their street on the way home. Point out that it might be on a special sign quite low down, or high up on the side of a building. Perhaps they can find out if the street is named at both ends.

Activity
Show the children envelopes which have been addressed to the school. Talk about the address and why it is necessary to have one; how it is vital to the post person if they are to know where to deliver the mail; that people will know that letters they have posted will get to the right place. Identify the street, the town, village or area, the county if appropriate, and the postcode.

Give each child an envelope on which is written their own address. In groups, if possible, identify the different parts of the address. Can they spot the number? Whose is the highest; the lowest? Perhaps some houses have a name or are part of a block of flats. Does everyone live on a street? Perhaps theirs is a road, a lane, an avenue and so on. Does everyone live in the same town or village? Identify the postcode. Ask the children who needs to know their address. They might suggest the post person, delivery people, friends visiting.

Show the children a large-scale map of the locality and help them to find the street where they live. For children living outside the immediate locality, indicate the direction of their house from the neighbourhood of the school.

2

Where do I live?

Recording
Give the children photocopiable page 28 on which they can copy their address from the envelopes and complete the sentences.

Differentiation
Children:
- copy their address or parts of the address
- copy their address and complete sentences relating to their address
- write some parts of their address independently.

Plenary
Sort a selection of the envelopes according to the children's suggestions, perhaps grouping according to whether they have street, road, lane and so on, perhaps into high numbers – over 20, or low numbers – less than 20. Read out a random address and ask the child who lives there to identify it.

   Put the envelopes in a box where they are easily accessible so that children can use them to invent their own sorting or identification games.

Display
Give each child a sticker on which to write their name and then it can be positioned on the map to show where they live. Include any children living outside the locality by positioning their stickers towards the edge of the map, perhaps with an arrow to show the direction of their house.

ACTIVITY 4

GEOGRAPHY

HOW WE TRAVEL TO SCHOOL

How we travel to school				
by walking	by car	sometimes by walking	sometimes by car	by bus

Learning objective
To be aware that people have different ways of travelling to school.

Resources
Coloured drawing paper; A4 sheets, 'How we travel to school', for children to make their own graphs (see left); large sheet of paper for making a graph; pencils and crayons.

Preparation
Find pictures or models to represent methods of travelling to school such as a person walking, a car, a bus; cut out small pieces of different-coloured paper to represent each child's method of travelling.

Activity
Discuss ways of travelling short distances within the neighbourhood and ask the children to tell you how they get to school. Does anyone come on a camel? Express surprise that no one arrives by helicopter. Talk about finding out how many people travel by each method and get the children to form groups according to their method of reaching school – by walking, by bus, by car,

sometimes walking and sometimes by car, and so on. Ask which looks the biggest group, which the smallest. Do any groups look about the same size? Perhaps the children will suggest standing in lines to make counting easier. Give the first person in each line a picture or model to represent the method of transport and point out that they have made themselves into a graph.

Recording

Show the children how to make an individual graph of the class results using your prepared templates (see Resources). Encourage some children to use the computer to make their graph.

Differentiation

Children:
■ take part in constructing the large graph to show travelling methods (see Display)
■ create an individual graph by filling in columns on a prepared template
■ create own graph, possibly using a computer.

Plenary

When the graph has been completed (see Display), ask relevant questions, with the children using the graph to find the information. For example, do those living furthest away from school always come by car? How do those living nearest to school travel? Talk about the advantages and disadvantages of walking and being driven to school. People who walk are exercising their bodies which is a good thing, yet being driven can be quicker which could be important if time is short. Point out that perhaps the children notice more things if they are walking to school.

Display

Make a large permanent graph by giving each child a colour-coded piece of paper, perhaps green for walking, red for car travellers and so on, on which they can write their name and perhaps do a drawing to represent their way of travelling to school.

ACTIVITY 5

FINDING MY WAY HOME

GEOGRAPHY

Learning objective

To observe the main features on the journey between school and home and to describe and represent the route.

Resources

Large-scale maps and aerial photographs of the locality; photocopiable page 29; pencils and crayons.

Preparation

Make a simplified large-scale map of the immediate area. Decide when to prepare the children for this activity and how long to give them to collect the information.

2

Where do I
live?

Activity

Remind the children on several occasions as they leave school that you want them to look carefully at the route they take to get home. Which way will they turn as they leave the school gates? What do they look for along the way which shows them which direction to go? How do they recognise their own street? Do they always go the same way? Can they remember the sequence of features they pass as they journey home? For example, leave school – look out for the post office – next turn the corner – then find the bus shelter – after that there is the newsagents, and so on. Provide the children with the photocopiable page, which will help them to focus on their journey home. For any children with a long journey, suggest they concentrate on the first part of their route home which includes the immediate neighbourhood of the school. Tell the children they can try out a map on the reverse of the page, if they wish.

When the children have had the opportunity to make their observations, show them a large-scale map of the locality. (This could be the map used in activity 3 with the stickers representing each child's address.) Choose a child who lives relatively close to the school to trace their route. Talk about the roads and any noticeable buildings or features. Encourage the child to talk about the features he or she looks out for to know they are going in the right direction. How do they recognise their street? Allow other children to trace their routes, perhaps in small groups. Can any of the children find their route on the aerial photograph?

Recording

Tell the children that you want them to use the information they have collected to draw a map showing the route they take to get home. Explain that they will need to show the roads and paths they use as well as drawing some of the buildings and features they see. Encourage them to mark in the safe places they use to cross roads. Show them how to choose a colour to mark the route itself and make a simple key to explain what the coloured line represents.

Differentiation

Children:
■ collect information with help and draw a simple map of their journey home
■ produce a map showing their route and including some details
■ produce a detailed map showing relevant features and their route home and make use of a key.

Plenary

In pairs or groups, allow the children to show their maps and talk about the route they take. Do any of them have a similar journey? Do other children go home to the same street as they do? Is there one feature a lot of people use to help them recognise their way home?

Display

Mark in some of the routes on the large map, using different colours, and provide a key.

Photocopiable

This is my house

roof

walls

door

windows

chimney

steps

porch

garage

Look carefully at the outside of your house. Draw what you see.

SCHOLASTIC

GEOGRAPHY

My address

Write your name and address on this envelope.

_____

_____

_____

_____

_____

The number of my house is _____

The name of my road is _____

_____

The place where I live is _____

_____

My postcode is _____

Someone who needs to know my address is _____

_____

_____

■SCHOLASTIC

GEOGRAPHY

Finding my way home

Which way do you go when you leave the school gates?

_____

Which buildings do you pass?

What are the names of the streets you travel along?

If you walk, which roads do you cross?

_____

_____

SCHOLASTIC

Section 3

Buildings and features round about

FOCUS

GEOGRAPHY
■ taking a closer look at the area around the school
■ extending observation of buildings and features of the immediate environment
■ understanding the importance and range of buildings in the area
■ experience of fieldwork
■ work with maps and plans

ART AND DESIGN
■ observational drawings
■ using symbols in design to represent buildings
■ practice in using a range of tools and techniques
■ working together to create a design for a work of art

RE
■ the church as a special building

ACTIVITY 1

GEOGRAPHY   ART & DESIGN

WHAT CAN WE SEE IN THE STREETS AROUND OUR SCHOOL?

Learning objectives
To recognise common and special features and buildings in the neighbourhood; to identify what different buildings are used for and make drawings from observation, noting shape and pattern.

Resources
Photographs, postcards, newspaper pictures and so on of features of interest in the area surrounding the school; clipboards; paper; pencils and crayons.

Preparation
Plan a walk around the neighbourhood; check out an ideal route and find out where there are safe places to stop and observe. Look out for relevant and interesting buildings such as the town hall, library, medical centre as well as features like a postbox, traffic island, park gates. Decide whether the children will work in groups or as a class. Depending on the situation, decide which particular building or buildings the children will draw or whether you will give them the opportunity to choose.

Take photographs of some of the features, landmarks and buildings beforehand. Build up a collection of photographs and postcards of the neighbourhood for the children to use during the activity including important buildings which they might not get to see on their walk.

Activity

Prepare the children for their walk around the neighbourhood (see Fieldwork opportunities, page 9). Suggest suitable clothing; talk about behaviour, especially towards people they might meet, and emphasise safety concerns. Explain that you will be recognising different buildings and looking out for interesting features. Refer to buildings or parts of buildings which the children might have seen from the school grounds (section 1, activity 1, page 10) or on their journey home (section 2, activity 5, page 25) when they might have had a different or closer view.

Take the children along the planned route, pointing out interesting features if appropriate, and stop at a pre-arranged spot. If there are several buildings in view, ask the children if they know what any of them are for. Are there any shops? If so, what do the shops sell? What are the other buildings used for? Is it possible to tell from the outside?

Focus on the building you want the children to draw. Ask questions to encourage careful observations. How many storeys high is the building? Do windows take up most of the front? What shape is the roof? Are there any patterns, perhaps around the windows or doors, or letters on signs which give people information? What are the main colours of the building?

Give the children time to make an observational drawing of the building. Explain that they need a quick but careful sketch which will remind them of the building and its parts when they are back at school, not a very detailed drawing which would take a long time to do. Suggest they work in three stages, looking first at the shape of the building and its roof, tracing the outline with a finger to help. Is the shape a square or perhaps a rectangle? Is it tall or wide? Can the roof be seen? Is it a special shape? Next, look at the features such as the windows and doors and their size in relation to the rest of the building. Add them to the drawing along with any chimneys, aerials, flag poles and so on. Finally focus on any decoration or other details such as brickwork, tiles and paint effects, sketching a small sample to serve as a reminder.

Also, during the walk, draw the children's attention to some of the features of the locality such as signposts, a statue, lamp-posts, a war memorial, traffic island, telephone box or bus shelter. Encourage them to look upwards as well as at eye level. If the location is convenient, ask the children to draw two or three features they can see.

Recording

Back at school, the children can improve their sketches if necessary and then write headings, words or sentences to go with their drawings. If it was not possible to make observational drawings, help the children to draw a building and some of the features they have seen, either from memory or photographs. If appropriate, encourage the children to write relevant sentences to accompany their drawings: *I know this is the bakery because... This signpost shows the way to...*

Differentiation

Children:
■ sketch a building or feature from observation and write a relevant heading
■ make an observational sketch of a building, considering shape, features and detail and writing a descriptive sentence
■ produce an accurate observational sketch of a building with accompanying explanatory sentences.

3

Buildings
and
features
round
about

Plenary

Encourage the children to remind each other of what they saw when they were on their walk. Talk about things which were tall or high up and things which were seen lower down. What did they see only one of and was there something of which there were many? Which features do the children see regularly, perhaps on their way home? Refer to previous work, if any of the buildings can be seen from the school grounds. Use the postcards to create identification and sorting games.

Display

Use the children's sketches together with photographs to make a montage of buildings and features.

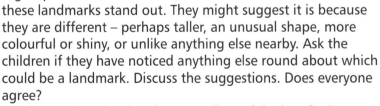

ACTIVITY 2

GEOGRAPHY

LOOKING AT LANDMARKS

Learning objective

To be aware of landmarks in the neighbourhood and their importance when finding your way about.

Resources

Aerial photographs of the immediate area as well as those of a well-known place the children might have visited; photographs of local landmarks; a large-scale map of the locality; pencils and crayons.

Preparation

If possible, arrange a walk on which children can find their way by looking out for landmarks. Take photographs of local landmarks. Prepare a simple large-scale map of the streets nearby and a smaller copy which can be photocopied for the children's use. Choose a few landmark buildings or features and represent these by symbols on stickers to use in conjunction with the large map.

Activity

Talk about what a landmark is – something that stands out and is easily seen. Introduce the idea that some of the features of the local area are landmarks, suggesting a particular building, a chimney, a pylon, a group of trees, and so on. Then ask the children what makes

these landmarks stand out. They might suggest it is because they are different – perhaps taller, an unusual shape, more colourful or shiny, or unlike anything else nearby. Ask the children if they have noticed anything else round about which could be a landmark. Discuss the suggestions. Does everyone agree?

Point out how landmarks are really useful when finding your way. Tell the children how you yourself use a particular landmark to get to school or a certain shop. Find out if there is any feature the children use. How do they know when they are near the park, for example? What do they look out for? Perhaps they do not realise that they are relying on landmarks.

Show the children the large map and explain which part of the neighbourhood it represents by pointing out some of the familiar streets. Ask the children which landmark buildings and features are in this area. Put stickers on the map to represent

CURRICULUM LINKS ages 5–7: Around our school

the landmarks as the discussion proceeds. Trace one or two routes along the streets, referring to the landmarks.

Recording
Provide the children with a simple outline of the local streets, on which they can draw landmarks. On the map they can plot a route for a visitor walking from one place to another. Some children might be sufficiently confident to draw their own map and add landmarks.

Differentiation
Children:
- recognise and draw landmarks on a simple map
- draw and label familiar landmarks on a simple map
- draw a simple map of the locality, putting in landmarks and tracing a particular route.

Plenary
Encourage the children to ask each other directions from one place to another. This can be done orally from memory or using one of their prepared maps. Talk about famous landmarks the children know – perhaps Big Ben, the Angel of the North, and so on.

Display
Create a wall display or make up an album of local landmarks using photographs and the children's work about their locality. Extend this to famous landmarks and include holiday postcards.

GEOGRAPHY

ART & DESIGN

ACTIVITY 3

WHAT ARE BUILDINGS FOR?

Learning objective
To emphasise the need for a variety of buildings in the locality and begin to relate design with function in a building.

Resources
Card for chart; paper; pencils and crayons.

Preparation
Mark out a chart (see right) with the names of the buildings the children will talk about. List the buildings down the left-hand side, with spaces to the right for drawing in the symbols during the activity. These might include the town hall, leisure centre, football stadium, church, post office, police station and library. The names of the buildings can be covered over until each one is discussed in turn. If possible, arrange a visit to look at the interior of a local building such as the town hall or library to understand its function and the purposes of different areas within the building.

building	symbol
library	
post office	
leisure centre (swimming pool)	
church	

Activity
Begin by asking the children why we need a school building. Their suggestions might include – a place where children can learn new things, do exciting projects, dance, play instruments, and so on. Point out that the building shelters the children as they work and play, keeps their books clean, prevents things getting wet or blown about, keeps them warm in the winter and cool in the summer, and keeps everyone safe.

Move on to discuss other buildings, especially those in the immediate locality with which the children are familiar. For each building, briefly describe its purpose and encourage the children to suggest a relevant symbol to represent it on the chart. For example, the library (purpose – a place where you can go to read and borrow books), can be represented by a pile or shelf of books. Fill in the chart with the children's suggestions for symbols as you go along.

If a visit to a particular building can be arranged, the children can see for themselves its purpose and the use of specific areas within the main building such as an entrance or reception area, staff area, the part where the public are allowed, and so on. Otherwise draw on the experience of children who have visited any of these buildings or ask what they expect the inside of a particular building to be like.

Recording
Ask the children to create designs using symbols to represent the function of two different buildings. The designs could be used for a rug or curtain fabric to enhance the buildings, and the children can use several different symbols to make their designs more interesting. Ask the children to write a sentence to go with each design to show where the rug or fabric is intended to be used.

Differentiation
Children:
■ match a symbol to a building and use this to create a design
■ choose symbols to represent a building and include these in a design
■ create their own symbols to represent a building and produce a relevant design.

Plenary
The children can identify the buildings represented by each other's designs and comment on the effectiveness of the designs. Which symbols are easily recognisable and which are the ones everyone will know? Is a simple design easier to recognise than one with a lot of detail?

Display
Display the children's rug/fabric designs in a temporary way while they are admired and discussed. Ask some children to reproduce particularly striking symbols to make a border for the display about buildings.

ACTIVITY 4

MAKING A WORK OF ART

ART & DESIGN

Learning objective
To collaborate in making a work of art (mural, plaque or table-top covering) which represents, through symbols and patterns, a familiar local building.

Resources
Material from which a tile can be moulded or cut out and a relief design created, such as clay or similar material, or papier mâché; tools for working with clay for rolling, engraving, scraping, carving – also improvised tools such as plastic cutlery, combs, old paintbrushes and so on; moulds for shaping the tiles which could be rectangular or square plastic or recycled

paper food trays, or specially made wooden frames about 15cm square (alternatively, templates can be used for shaping the tiles); examples of relief patterning in ceramics or carved wood; clay glazes and liquid clay (slips); paints; PVA glue; paper; pencils and crayons.

Preparation

In this activity each child creates an individually designed tile. The tiles arranged together create one or more panels which communicate the purpose and features of a building the children know well. Decide upon which familiar building in the locality offers the best opportunities for the children to represent in symbols and pattern as a 'work of art'. For example, the library – patterns made by rows of books, shelves, pages, letters, computer equipment; leisure centre – waves, swimming aids, clothing, training shoes, ball games, exercise equipment; church (after the visit described in section 4, see page 39) – shape of the building, features within and without, services.

Decide on size, final position and the material and method the children will use to create their tiles. Tiles made from clay can be moulded using a frame or shaped container or cut out using a suitable template. When finished, they can be arranged on a flat surface such as a low table or cupboard top, or on a slightly tilted wooden board. Alternatively, they can be glued with strong adhesive onto a suitable wall display board. Tiles made from moulded papier mâché can be stapled or glued to a display board to make a mural.

Next, decide how the class will be organised. For example, children can discuss ideas for their design in pairs. Then two pairs can get together to consider how four tiles might look. Two groups of four can then share ideas again, trying to get a feeling for the overall design.

Consider whether each group of eight will represent the whole of the building or a different part of the building. For instance, with the leisure centre, different groups can focus on the swimming aspect, sports involving balls, exercises, and the building itself.

Plan the sessions in which the children will be involved. The activity can take place in two parts:
- introduction, discussion and drawing plans
- creating the tiles, with groups taking turns if space and equipment is limited.

Prepare the materials. If clay is to be used, find out how much is required for the moulds or template being used and roll into balls of this quantity. If using papier mâché, make up an appropriate quantity.

Activity

Part 1: discussing and designing

Explain to the children that together they will be creating a large piece of artwork, a 'work of art' which will tell people about a particular building. Describe the building you have decided upon. Tell the children that by looking at the design people will know which building it is, what it is used for and perhaps what it is like inside and out. Symbols, patterns and shapes will be used to give clues about the building.

Move on to explain to the children how they will be involved individually and as a class, that each of them will design a tile out of clay (or papier mâché). Put together, the tiles will give a bigger and better impression of the building. Describe how the artwork will be textural as well as visual, that it will be interesting to feel as well as to look at. Show the class a piece of ceramic ware or decorative ornament which has a relief pattern, so that the children can begin to understand what is expected of them. Talk briefly about how the effects will be achieved but save details for a later demonstration. Remind the children of any previous artwork they have done involving modelling, engraving and printing.

Suggest the children talk about their ideas with a partner for a few minutes, perhaps making some rough sketches to show each other what they feel would make good symbols and representative patterns.

When each pair has had an opportunity to discuss, put them together with another pair so that four children can share ideas and suggestions. If collaboration is proving successful, put together two groups of four with the children working together towards producing a panel of eight tiles. During this process, encourage the children to think of their design as individual to themselves while becoming part of the whole artwork.

Provide each child with an outline of the shape and size their finished tile will be, on which they can attempt their design. Ensure the children include their initials discreetly in their design. When the designs have been completed, cut out the shapes so that the paper patterns can be arranged as a panel. Help each group to decide how the tiles fit together in a pleasing way, perhaps rearranging and rotating the paper tiles to achieve the effect which satisfies the group. Although the completed tiles might evolve differently in the making process, this practice the children have in assembling the panel will help them to understand what the completed work of art will be like.

Part 2: creating the tile

To make the most efficient use of space and equipment, groups can take turns to work on their tiles. Demonstrate how to roll out the ball of clay to a thickness of no less than one

centimetre, cutting, joining and pressing into the mould with fingers and appropriate tools. Alternatively a cutting tool can be used to shape the clay using a template such as a plastic shape or ready-made tile.

Next, demonstrate the techniques which can be used to achieve a relief pattern, building up using a clay and water mix, and carving, making indentations and printing using specific clay tools as well as improvised equipment.

If papier mâché is used, show how it can be pressed directly and evenly into the mould to make a firm base and then built up and modelled with extra material, card and different types of paper, as well as patterned with pressing effects.

Then give the children each a ball of clay and a selection of tools so that they can make their own tile and create a design. Until the decoration of each tile is complete, keep it covered with a damp cloth and protect it in a tightly fastened plastic bag.

Finished clay tiles can be coloured using paint mixed with PVA glue. If a kiln is available, tiles can be painted with special clay glazes before firing. Papier mâché tiles, when completely dry, can be painted and then coated with diluted PVA glue to make them water resistant.

When all the tiles for one panel are complete, give the group the opportunity to arrange and rearrange them until the children are satisfied with the effect achieved. Clay tiles can be displayed on a horizontal or slightly tilted surface or glued with strong adhesive to a display board where they can be easily seen by the children, while papier mâché tiles can be stapled or glued to a vertical display board.

Differentiation

Children:

■ design and create a tile using appropriate patterns and symbols and a range of tools and techniques

■ design and create an individual tile using a range of tools and techniques and work collaboratively to produce a panel

■ collaborate to create a panel of tiles, using relevant symbols and experimenting with a range of tools and a variety of techniques.

Plenary

Admire the completed panels, perhaps arranging an unveiling ceremony. Invite comments from the children on their own and others' panels. How well did the groups work together? Was the effect what they expected? Did they change anything along the way? Did their panel turn out better than they thought, or not so well? What is the reaction of other classes in the school, parents, visitors?

Perhaps the children's comments together with explanations about how they produced their work of art could be communicated to parents at a special assembly or parents' evening.

RE

ACTIVITY 5

WHY ARE CHURCHES DIFFERENT?

Learning objective
To be aware that churches can be different in appearance from other buildings and that they have a special use.

Resources
Pictures and video featuring a range of different of churches; photocopiable page 38; pencils and crayons.

Preparation
List key vocabulary such as *church, chapel, cathedral, mosque, famous, spire, tower* and so on for children to refer to when recording.

Activity
Ask the children to remind each other how they recognise the local church, which was probably the one identified in previous activities (section 1, activity 4, page 14). It might be characterised by the material from which it is built, for example stone. Perhaps by its position – for example, it is set within a churchyard on a hill. Perhaps it has a tower, spire or dome.

Ask the children if they know of any other churches and whether they have different exterior features. Make the children aware that there are other types of religious buildings and show them pictures of cathedrals, a mosque, synagogue, chapels, modern church, non-conformist church, and so on. Show pictures or a video featuring churches. Talk about the visible decorative exterior features which many churches have that often make them stand out. Remind the children about landmarks and talk about any famous churches they know, perhaps a nearby cathedral or Westminster Abbey.

Talk about how churches are different from homes, that they are usually larger and hold many people at a time, that people do not live in them. Explain to the children the special purpose of a church, and that it is very important to the people who go there to worship, and for special services. Explain that it is because people want their church to be special that it often has features which are quite different from other buildings.

Recording
Children can draw a church they know or copy one they have seen in a picture or photograph, and label the familiar external features such as porch, tower or spire, arched windows, large doorway, decorated windows, symbols of crosses, and so on. Alternatively, they can use their knowledge of churches to design the exterior of a church for themselves, giving it some of the features they know. Children can use the photocopiable page to draw and label their drawing of a church, writing a sentence describing some of the features included. The vocabulary list can be used for reference when labelling and sentence writing.

Differentiation
Children:
■ make a simple drawing of a church, identifying some of its external features
■ draw and label the external features of a church and explain why it is a special place
■ make a detailed, labelled drawing of the external features of a church with accompanying sentences explaining why it is a special place.

Plenary
Ask the children to remind each other why people who belong to a church like the building to be a special place. Talk about some of the different features of the churches they have drawn.

Churches are different

porch tower spire doorway decoration carvings window cross churchyard walls roof

This church _____

_____

_____

Visiting a church

FOCUS

RE
■ anticipating the church visit
■ impressions of the interior of the church
■ features and artefacts inside the church
■ people using the church
■ importance of the church within the local community

ART AND DESIGN
■ observational drawing

Preparation for section 4

The activities in this section all arise from a visit to a local Christian church. Contact the minister or a church worker to find out about access and permission required to enter the building and then make a preliminary visit. Familiarise yourself with the interior of the building and check out the features and artefacts you will want the children to see. Much will depend on the age and size of the building. Take photographs if possible. (See Getting started, page 7.)

Locate any booklets or information boards which are often available to tell visitors about the building. Otherwise enlist the help of a church worker to provide information. Request permission if you would like the children to make rubbings inside the church.

Look carefully at the interior of the building itself:
■ roof – height, construction features, decoration, materials
■ windows – shapes, patterns, pictures, stained glass
■ pillars – size, position, number, materials
■ doorway – position, shape, materials.
If the church is of a modern design, look for features which emphasise its simplicity.

Locate the important features in the church:
■ altar – the holy table which is the centre for the worship and where there might be candlesticks, a cross and flowers
■ pulpit – the raised platform from where the minister talks to the people
■ lectern – the place where the heavy Bible is rested and from which people read during the services
■ crosses – symbols of Christianity which can be found in many parts of the church
■ candles – symbols of light, to indicate the presence of God
■ hassocks – special cushions for use when kneeling to say prayers
■ font – the place where babies and sometimes adults are taken to be baptised
■ features specific to the church such as statues, memorials and so on.
Prepare a vocabulary list of key words.

4

Visiting a church

Organise the children into small groups for the visit, each with a responsible adult as leader with whom they should stay on the journey and when working in the church.

Then decide how the children will use the church, which parts they will need to see, where they will sit when listening, observing and drawing.

The visit can be planned in three stages:

1. Arrange for the children to sit quietly in the church to absorb the special atmosphere.
2. Plan a tour of the church so that all children see the important features and artefacts.
3. Organise close examination of selected features and artefacts.

(Each group could concentrate on different features within the church.)

It may be appropriate for the minister or church worker to invite the children, either personally or by letter to visit their church. Make sure the day of the visit is suitable to both parties and explain exactly what the children will be doing when inside the church. If a church worker is available to welcome the visitors and guide the party around, provide a list of the features and artefacts you want the children to focus on.

Inform parents by letter of the day and time of the visit to the church, explaining any special arrangements and advising on suitable clothing to be worn. Use this opportunity to request any extra help needed. Provide any special instructions regarding the journey. Prepare simple instructions for helpers to ensure they know what is expected of them and to give them confidence to help the children as appropriate.

ACTIVITY 1

RE

INTRODUCING THE VISIT TO THE CHURCH

Learning objective
To know that a church is a special place for Christians.

Resources
Photographs of the church to be visited.

Preparation
See above.

Activity
One or two days before the visit, tell the children that they will be visiting a Christian church. Perhaps you can identify it as the one they have focused on in earlier activities (section 1, activity 4, page 14; section 3, activity 5, page 37). It might be a local landmark or a building that can be seen from the school. Ask the children how they might recognise a church from the outside. Perhaps it has a tower or spire; stands in a churchyard. Refer to any photographs showing the outside of the church.

Find out if anyone has been inside the church and what was the reason. There might be children from families who attend this church regularly. Others might have been to special services at Christmas, Easter or harvest time, or to a wedding or baptism. Use this opportunity for the children to share their knowledge and experiences. Ask what they noticed about the inside of the building; any unusual features; about the people involved in the services. Perhaps some of the children will tell you they have been to a different church. If so, ask them what features they remember. Will they see similar features in all churches? If no one has visited the church, find out what the children expect to see inside the building.

Explain that the church is a very special place for Christians, that it is where they meet to worship their God. They pray, sing, listen to talks and read the Bible.

Explain the reason for the visit, that the children will be able to find out what a Christian church is like inside. They will be able to look closely at the special things inside the church and discover how some of them are used. Build up a sense of anticipation, so that the children know that they are going to be visiting somewhere special.

Discuss appropriate behaviour for inside the church such as moving about carefully, speaking softly and generally being respectful. Talk about meeting people in the church, perhaps people who have come to enjoy the quiet atmosphere where they can think without everyday interruptions. Perhaps the cleaners or flower arrangers will be busy. Prepare the children to meet anyone who you have arranged to talk to them and show them round.

Tell the children about the activities they will work on in the church so that they will have a clear understanding of what is expected of them.

ACTIVITY 2

FIRST IMPRESSIONS

Learning objective
To be aware of the atmosphere inside the church and begin to understand why it is such a special place for Christians.

Resources
For each group leader: a clipboard; paper with a heading 'What does it feel like in this church?'; pen.

Preparation
On the day of the visit, remind the children of their behaviour and responsibilities. Make sure each child is aware of which adult is caring for them. Remind them about travelling safely and behaving responsibly on the way. Explain that they will be expected to complete several tasks while in the church. Give them any special instructions about returning to school.

Activity
Take the children into the church and allow them to sit quietly for a few minutes to take in the atmosphere and look around. Then the group leaders should ask the children what they are thinking and how they feel about being in the church. Encourage soft speaking so as to preserve the atmosphere. To help the children remember how they felt, suggest the group leaders jot down the children's first impressions of the interior of the church, without prompting to begin with. Each child should be encouraged to make a contribution. Quotes can be single words, a collection of words, phrases or sentences. If necessary, the leaders can quietly ask questions to encourage ideas: where is the brightest part of the church? What makes it brighter than the rest? What colours will you remember when you are back at school? How do you feel in the church? (Cold, warm, happy, peaceful?) If you close your eyes what sounds and smells do you notice? Let the group leaders spend about 10–15 minutes collecting this information.

Visiting a church

4

Visiting a church

RE   ART & DESIGN

ACTIVITY 3

SPECIAL THINGS INSIDE THE CHURCH

Learning objectives
To identify features and artefacts inside the church and begin to understand their significance to Christian worship; to encourage careful observation of decoration and artefacts within the building.

Resources
Clipboards; paper; pencils and crayons.

Preparation
Make sure you can inform the children about the important features in the church (see Preparation for section 4, page 39).

Activity
Depending on the space within the church and the number of people involved, take the children around the church as a class or in small groups. During the tour of the interior of the church point out any interesting features of the building such as a huge heavy wooden door, stone pillars, a high decorative roof. Show the children the parts of the church which are important in Christian worship: the altar, pulpit, lectern, hassocks, candles and images of the cross. Briefly explain the use and relevance of these things to Christians.

Identify different areas of the church. Point out where the minister sits during a service, the spaces for the choir, where the congregation assembles, the porch, the aisles and the font where baptisms take place. Explain which parts are the most important and link the artefacts with the activities of the church. Give the children the opportunity to ask any questions relating to what they have seen in the church and the way things are used.

After the tour of the church, ask the children to observe carefully two of the things they have seen inside the church with a view to making a detailed drawing of each. Explain that the things they are looking at are very special to the people of the church and great care must be taken not to spoil or damage anything. Provide the children with clipboards and drawing materials and show them where you want them to sit. It might be appropriate for each group to draw different features to obtain a wide range of drawings to discuss and display when back in the classroom. As the children are making their drawings, encourage them to look carefully at any pattern or decoration they see and perhaps make a note of the colours.

Encourage the children to experience the different textures of stone, polished wood and metal by touching sensitively. If permission has been obtained, some children can help to make a selection of rubbings to show the range of textures present in the church – perhaps the wood of the door, the decoration on stonework or an inscription on metal.

Before leaving, make sure the children thank any church workers who have helped them.

RE   ART & DESIGN

ACTIVITY 4

BACK AT SCHOOL

Learning objective
To recap on why a church is a special place for Christians and to reinforce knowledge of the internal features of a church.

Resources
Children's quotes about their first impressions of the church (see Preparation).

Preparation
Collect together the group leaders' completed sheets ('What does it feel like in this church?')
from activity 2.

Activity
Spend some time reading the children's quotes and talking about their first impressions of
the inside of the church. Was it as they expected? Did anything surprise them? Did they enjoy
the experience of being in the church? How did those children who had not been inside the
church before feel? Conclude that the peaceful atmosphere of a church is very different from
many other buildings and that this makes it a special place for Christians to worship.

Discuss the interesting parts of the building which the children observed in activity 3 and
look at the drawings. Then talk about the furniture and artefacts relating to Christian
worship. Get the children to remind each other of the purpose in the church of the altar,
lectern, pulpit, cross and so on. Use their drawings to illustrate the discussion.

Talk about the events and activities which take place in the church and refer to pictures and
photographs of weddings, baptisms and other services. Remind the children how Christian
people like their church to be special and look beautiful. Mention the cleaners, flower
arrangers and organist or other musicians. Briefly talk about the church as a part of the
community, where people can meet together, celebrate Christian occasions and make friends.

Recording
Ask the children to record their visit to the church in sentences and pictures. Provide a list of
key words and, if appropriate, provide prompts such as sentence starters for the children to
complete: *The pulpit is where... On the lectern... People use the hassocks...* Encourage the
children to describe how things in the church are important to Christians in their services.

Differentiation
Children:
■ copy or write words or sentences to describe the drawings they have made of the things in
the church which interested them
■ describe in sentences and with drawings their visit to the church, referring to features and
artefacts relevant to Christian worship
■ write a detailed account of the visit to the church,
explaining the significance of some of the features and
artefacts in Christian worship.

Plenary
When all the work about the church is complete, remind
the children that the church they have visited is a special
place where Christians worship. Ask them to tell each other
what they think makes the church special. Point out that
other people attend different types of churches and
worship in different ways.

Display
Use photographs, pictures and the children's drawings to
create a wall display about the church. Arrange the
children's quotes in speech bubbles around the display or
collect the quotes together in a book. If the work created
in section 3 relates to the church, make it the focal point of
the display.

Arrange a special assembly or parents' afternoon when
the children can show their work and talk about their visit.

<table>
<tr><td>

Section 5

</td><td>

What is it like around here?

</td></tr>
</table>

GEOGRAPHY

FOCUS

GEOGRAPHY
- human influence on the local environment
- activities by people in the streets of the neighbourhood
- personal responsibilities within the community
- children expressing opinions
- observational activities
- mapwork
- opportunities for fieldwork

GEOGRAPHY

ACTIVITY 1

WHAT HAPPENS IN OUR STREETS?

Learning objective
To become aware of the human activity within the surrounding area.

Resources
Photographs and a video film of people in the streets; photocopiable page 51; paper; pencils and crayons.

Preparation
Take photographs of local street scenes which show people engaged in everyday activities. Make a vocabulary list of these activities such as *shopping, cleaning, digging, jogging* and so on. Prepare the children for this activity by asking them, perhaps over a weekend or on their way to school, to notice the sort of things the people they see in the street are doing.

Activity
Ask the children in turn what they have noticed people are doing in the streets round about. They might have seen people shopping, going to work, post being delivered, roadworkers, people cycling, gardening, cleaning windows. Try to discuss a variety of activities including those which are especially typical of the neighbourhood, which could be farming, building, delivering goods to shops or shopping activities. Build up a collection of verbs which describe the activities such as *shopping, delivering, sweeping, meeting* and so on. Encourage the children to add to the list over a period of days.

Discuss which type of people the children might see and if they all do similar things. Is it always older people who are walking dogs? Who is doing the shopping? What time of day do people get their post in the area? What activities take place in the morning? In the afternoon? When does the crossing patrol do his or her job? What activity takes place only once a week? What do the children think are the most common activities? Make a list of five common activities and another list showing those which occur infrequently.

Recording

Provide the children with copies of photocopiable page 51 on which they can represent two street scenes, one illustrating activities they see often and one those they see less often. Suggest they include three activities in each of their street scenes and write words or sentences to describe the activities using the vocabulary list. Extra ideas can be continued on the reverse of the page. Alternatively, some children can write sentences about the activities they have seen around the area.

Differentiation

Children:
■ represent some activities of people in the streets of their neighbourhood with pictures and captions
■ draw and write simple sentences about a range of activities which occur in the neighbourhood
■ make a list showing a range of activities in the neighbourhood, drawing and writing sentences to distinguish between frequent and less frequent occurrences.

Plenary

Devise a game in which a child mimes one of the activities and the others have to identify which activity it is. Encourage the children to ask each other questions to help solve the mime. Would you see this in the streets every day? Does this happen at the same time every day? Is this an activity which only happens now and again?

Display

Arrange the photographs of the activities with appropriate captions to show what happens in the area. Display the vocabulary list of verbs, perhaps colour-coding to show the most and least frequent activities.

ACTIVITY 2

GEOGRAPHY

NICE OR NASTY?

Learning objective

To be aware that human activity can have a positive or negative influence on the neighbourhood.

Resources

Photographs and video film of parts of the neighbourhood which could be described as 'nice' and as 'nasty'; paper; pencils and crayons.

Preparation

Take photographs of the attractive and less attractive areas of the neighbourhood. Nice places could include a green area, public bench, clump of trees, corner of a park, an attractive shop front such as a well-stocked greengrocer's window, a place where there is an interesting view. Nasty places might show accumulations of litter, graffiti, something damaged, and so on. Focus on public places rather than residential areas where the children might have their homes.

5

What is it like around here?

Activity

Ask the children about their favourite places in the locality, places where they like to go. They may talk about a park, play area, shopping centre or path where they can walk. Move on to places where they do not like to go, perhaps areas which they and their family avoid. They might talk about disliking the litter and dirt, not wanting to see damage, feeling unsafe.

Discuss what makes a place nice. Is it likely to be clean – perhaps there are trees and flowers, places to sit, somewhere safe to play, things to look at, somewhere you would want to go, a pleasant place to be? Talk about why the place is like this. What sort of people look after it? Is it the council, those who live nearby, everyone? Perhaps it is respected by people and they avoid spoiling it. Decide whether there are enough of these places locally.

Talk about places which are the opposite of nice. What makes them nasty and unpleasant? Have the children noticed litter, dog dirt, damage to trees or seats and so on? Perhaps there is graffiti on walls and signs. Discuss how all these things spoil the environment and make the area unattractive. Why are there places like this? Perhaps some people do not care and do not think about keeping a place nice. What are the children's opinions? Do they think there are many nasty spots in the neighbourhood? Are there more nice than nasty places? In the discussion, beware of associating the term *nasty* with the areas where children might live; focus on public areas instead.

Emphasise the part that people play in making an area a pleasant place to be. Highlight the children's own responsibility in helping to make the neighbourhood attractive by not dropping litter, by behaving sensibly and taking care not to damage trees and property when playing.

Recording

Ask the children to show on paper what they think makes a nasty place and a nice place. Some children will be able to write sentences explaining how places come to be nice or nasty.

Differentiation

Children:
■ represent nice and nasty places of their neighbourhood in their drawings, giving their opinions orally
■ represent nice and nasty places of their neighbourhood with drawings, giving their opinions in sentences
■ represent in detail the nice and nasty parts of the neighbourhood, writing relevant comments and opinions.

Plenary

Stress the part children can play in shaping their neighbourhood. Ask for suggestions for a code for others to follow: *Take litter home with you. Clean up after your dog. Don't trample on the flowers.*

Display

Arrange the photographs of nice and nasty places with appropriate headings, and print out the statements of the code with the title 'How to make... [name of neighbourhood] nicer'. Print out some of the children's comments to add to the display.

ACTIVITY 3

GEOGRAPHY

BUSY AND QUIET PLACES

Learning objectives

To be aware of differences between busy and quiet areas of the neighbourhood; to understand that other people's surroundings might differ from their own.

Resources

Photographs and video film of contrasting busy and quiet areas within the neighbourhood as well as pictures of other obviously quiet places such as the countryside and noticeably busy places like the centre of a city; photocopiable page 52; paper; pencils and crayons.

Preparation

If possible, arrange a walk to include a quiet and a busier part of the locality. Take photographs of these areas and arrange them for discussion.

Activity

Ask the children what makes a place busy. They might suggest lots of people, much noise, traffic, lots of things happening at once. Identify and list any such places close by and talk about what makes each a busy spot. Refer to the photographs taken in the locality.

Contrast these with quiet places. Ask the children where they could go to get away from busyness for a while. Where is it quiet and peaceful around here? Is there somewhere free from traffic with few people about? Make a class list of such places. If out on a walk, stop at a busy spot and then in a quieter place and record the things which describe each of these contrasting places. Otherwise, use photographs of the neighbourhood to contrast busy and quiet places.

Talk about enjoying being in a busy place for some of the time as well as enjoying more peaceful moments. Decide whether the area around the school is busy or quiet. Perhaps it has busy times and quieter times. Which children think they live in a quieter spot than the school? Do some live in a busier place?

Move on to talking about making a busy area safer. Highlight some local road safety issues. Ask how children can make sure they are safe where there is traffic about. Do they cross the roads carefully and at the safest places? Do they listen to advice from parents and teachers? Are there enough crossing places for people on the dangerously busy roads? Is parking a problem? Discuss how parked cars can be a danger to people trying to get across roads.

Briefly talk about being safe in busy and quiet places. Explain the need for young children to be with adults they know. Take the opportunity to remind them about the hazards of water, cliffs, getting lost, tractors and so on in the countryside.

Remind the children to be aware of strangers in both busy and quiet places and explain that traffic can be dangerous even in quieter places because people sometimes think they do not have to be so careful.

Recording

Ask the children to depict their ideas of a busy place and a quiet place by adding to the outlines on the photocopiable page, making one place quiet and one busy. Ask for ideas for each picture. How can the road be made busy? Perhaps the busy picture needs lots of

5

What is it like around here?

buildings and people. In the quiet picture the road will be a lane – there will be more trees, other plants, a few people and perhaps some wild animals. Suggest the children put themselves in each of their pictures doing an appropriate activity. Ask them to explain in words or sentences which type of place they prefer.

Differentiation
Children:
■ contrast busy and quiet places in their drawings
■ use drawings and sentences to contrast busy and quiet places and indicate preferences
■ use drawings and sentences to contrast busy and quiet places, expressing preferences and opinions clearly and in detail.

Plenary
Choose some areas of the neighbourhood and ask the children to tell you if they are busy or quiet. Can they think of spots which can sometimes be busy and at other times quiet? Where do they think it is always busy? In the middle of London? Where is it always quiet? At the top of a mountain? Where would they go to live if they liked a busy place? Where would they live if they liked quiet surroundings?

Display
Arrange photographs together with children's drawings and large headings emphasising the quiet and busy aspects of the locality.

ACTIVITY 4

HELP FOR VISITORS

GEOGRAPHY

Learning objective
To plan a route around the neighbourhood to give visitors a good impression of the area.

Resources
Large-scale maps of the area for reference; simple maps with keys to use as examples, such as those produced in tourist information leaflets; photocopies of a simple outline of the streets of the area; paper; pencils and crayons.

Preparation
Choose two suitable places within walking distance of each other to help the children plan a route which would give visitors a good impression of the area. Places could be a museum, factory, town hall, park and so on. Prepare and make copies of a simple outline map of the locality, naming the main streets of the area on which landmarks and interesting features can be added during the activity. Group the children into pairs for the activity to encourage collaboration.

Activity
Explain to the children that a group of people is soon to visit the neighbourhood. Tell them that the visitors would like to see two particular places of interest, and name the chosen places. The visitors will walk from one venue to another. Tell the children they will be working with a partner to plan the best route. It need not be the quickest route but should be interesting and take in the

most attractive parts of the area, avoiding any 'nasty' spots. (Refer to activity 2 of this section, page 45.)

First, show the children the map outline and ask questions to help them get their bearings: if this is the main road, where will the museum be? The town hall is halfway down the high street so where do you think it will be on the map? Talk about representing the landmarks on the map. Perhaps symbols or small drawings of buildings would be a good idea. Discuss the size of the symbols, which should not be too big or too small, and the importance of having a key. Refer to previous map work such as 'Finding my way home' (section 2, activity 5, page 25). Show the children examples of maps with symbols and a key – either one you have made or perhaps a simple map from a local tourist information leaflet.

Talk about choosing a route where there are other interesting features along the way which people can see, and how these can be shown as symbols. Remind the children how to represent a route using a coloured line which should be shown as part of the key. Give the pairs of children time to discuss a route before making their plan.

Recording

After the collaboration, each child should complete their own map. Emphasise that the finished map must look attractive and will need symbols and a key. Some children might like to devise a commentary, spoken or written, to guide the visitors around and give them extra information.

Differentiation

Children:
- plot a route on a map outline, using symbols to represent landmarks
- plot a route on a map outline, representing landmarks with symbols and devising a key
- plot a route on a map outline, make use of symbols and a key, and prepare a commentary describing the route.

Plenary

Admire the maps. Which do the children think will help the visitors the most? Do the maps give accurate information? Are they attractive? Will people like to use them? Are the symbols easy to understand? Is the key clear and helpful? If appropriate, photocopy the maps so that children can take a version home for visiting friends and relatives to try. Encourage feedback from home.

Display

To emphasise the value of the children's work, arrange the maps prominently, possibly where visitors to the school can see them. Write a short explanation so that the aim of the activity is clear.

ACTIVITY 5

GEOGRAPHY

CHANGES AROUND HERE

Learning objective

To notice changes in the locality and to be aware that changes have always happened and will continue to do so.

Resources
Photographs and drawings of the area in the past, particularly of the school and the surrounding streets; paper; pencils and crayons.

Preparation
If possible, organise a visit around the neighbourhood to look for changes which are occurring. Arrange for a photographer, perhaps a parent or older child, to take pictures of the children.

Activity
Begin by focusing on something locally that is changing – perhaps a new house being built or a shop being renovated. Ask the children if they have noticed any other changes as they travel to school. They might have seen new pavements being constructed, a garden being altered, a building demolished. Talk about whether, in the children's view, the changes are a good thing or not. Perhaps they are good for some people but not for others. Is there anything happening which is not good? Perhaps a park is being damaged, perhaps some rubbish has been dumped in the street. List the good and bad changes. Make a separate list of any changes on which the children cannot agree regarding whether they are good or bad.

Explain that changes are always happening and will continue to do so. Show old pictures of the school or a local street and discuss how things have changed. Talk about how interesting it is to be able to see what things were like, especially before the children were born. Arrange for the children to have photographs taken individually, or a class photograph, ideally beside a small tree in the school grounds. Each child could hold a favourite book or toy of the moment. Tell the children that these photos will be saved and available for them to see when they are ready to leave the school, probably in four or five years' time. Then they will be able to notice the changes which have taken place.

Recording
Mount the photographs, perhaps within an individual small folder, with space for the children to write some personal details including their name, the date, their age, where the picture was taken, what they were thinking of, and so on. If appropriate, children can record examples of changes they have noticed around the school or near their home, by drawing and writing.

Differentiation
Children:
- are aware and talk about changes in their neighbourhood
- notice changes and make comments, perhaps through drawing and writing
- give opinions about changes in their neighbourhood, using drawings or writing to record their comments.

Plenary
Explain to the children how important the photographic record of themselves and the surroundings will be in the future as changes are bound to happen. What are they sure will have changed? They will definitely have grown and will perhaps have a different hairstyle and another favourite toy. You could point out that the children will have learned much more, although you will not be able to tell this from the photograph. Decide if the surroundings will change. (The tree will have grown.)

Display
Arrange the photographs showing changes.

GEOGRAPHY

In our streets

We see these things happening most often.

We see these things happening not so often.

Photocopiable · GEOGRAPHY

Busy and quiet places

_____

_____

_____

Work and play

FOCUS

GEOGRAPHY

GEOGRAPHY
■ buildings and land in the locality providing opportunities for jobs and leisure
■ looking at some areas of work in the neighbourhood
■ leisure facilities locally
■ developing a sense of community
■ mapwork
■ making a survey

GEOGRAPHY

ACTIVITY 1

PEOPLE AT WORK

Learning objective
To understand that buildings and land in the neighbourhood provide people with jobs.

Resources
Photographs or video film of people doing jobs around the neighbourhood; two large pieces of card or paper for making lists and attaching photographs; Blu-Tack; photocopiable page 60; pencils and crayons.

Preparation
Have available photographs of local people at work in a variety of jobs, both indoors and outdoors, for example people working in shops and offices, a bank or health centre, a crossing patrol, police officer, traffic warden, and so on.

Activity
Remind the children that you come to school to do a job of work along with others including the rest of the teachers, lunchtime supervisors, cleaners and so on. The school provides work for people because lots of children live nearby and need a building in which to learn and be cared for.

Encourage the children to think of other buildings close by in the neighbourhood where there are people working. Perhaps there are shops, a factory, garage, public house, a library. Ask the children if there is a medical centre or cinema nearby where people work. Do the children have relatives or friends who work in these places? On a large piece

Leslie Garland Picture Library/alamy.com

of card or a sheet of paper, make a list of the jobs the children suggest, showing them the appropriate photographs as the discussion proceeds to help them visualise the work in question. Point out that these are indoor jobs. Attach the photographs with Blu-Tack and display them around the list.

Move on to discuss people who are working outside locally. Perhaps there are workers keeping the roads in good order, people busy at the scrapyard or recycling centre, groundsmen attending to the football pitch, farmers tending crops in the field. Emphasise the concept that the land is also providing people with jobs. Point out that small areas of land such as the local park provide work as well as bigger areas such as fields. Make a second list of jobs, explaining that these are outdoor types of work. Show the children the photographs and attach them to the card, placing them around the list.

Ask some of the children to tell you which kind of work they would like to try, giving their reasons: for example, *Lily and Tom would like to work at the cattery because they love animals; Sam and Mia think they would like jobs at the garage as they are interested in cars.*

Recording
Ask the children to write about which job they would most like to have and encourage them to include their reasons. Suggest they mention what sort of building they would work in. Perhaps they would be outside most of the time. What would they most like doing in their chosen job? What sort of people would they meet during the course of their work? Would they need any special clothing or tools? Provide the children with the photocopiable page to record this.

Differentiation
Children:
■ show with a drawing and words the job they would like to do
■ illustrate and write sentences describing a job they would like to do
■ write and illustrate a detailed account of a job they would like to do.

Plenary
Talk about what the most common jobs seem to be in the locality. What sort of jobs do most people do around where the children live? Can they think of jobs that cannot be done in the neighbourhood, such as deep-sea fishing, if situated away from the coast, or farming if in a big city? Remind the children that it is the buildings and the land which provide the work for the people.

Display
Display the two lists with photographs and the children's work.

ACTIVITY 2

THIS IS MY JOB

GEOGRAPHY

Learning objective
To appreciate and understand something of the work done by a person or people locally.

Resources
A camera; paper; pencils and crayons.

Preparation

Arrange for the children to meet a local working person who can suitably explain what they do. If possible, organise a visit to a safe workplace such as the library, dental surgery or health centre where the worker can show the children around the building in which they work. If more appropriate, invite into school a person who could talk about their work – perhaps a baker, restaurant worker or traffic warden. Talk to the person beforehand, explaining the things children may like to ask, for example where do you work? What time do you start? Do you wear special clothes? What is it you actually do? Is the work dangerous? What are the special skills you need? How many people work with you? Do they all do the same things? Explain also how long you would like the person to speak, and point out any problems which might arise. Encourage the worker to bring with them relevant artefacts or items of special clothing and perhaps demonstrate an aspect of their work.

Before the visit, tell the children that someone who works nearby is going to talk to them about their work. Explain that this will be very interesting and an opportunity for them and you to find out lots of information from an expert. Talk about the things they might find out from the visit. It might be appropriate to consider beforehand some questions which can be asked by individual children. If necessary, these can be rehearsed, but do allow for spontaneous queries which will arise. Explain how important it is to listen carefully to the visitor to avoid asking any questions that have already been answered.

Activity

On the day of the visit, establish where the visitor's workplace is and its position in relation to the school. Show the children a large-scale plan of the local area, perhaps the one they are familiar with from a previous activity (section 5, activity 4, page 48).

Introduce the person to the children and tell them to listen carefully to the talk before attempting to ask questions. Encourage the children to find out how many people there are at the workplace, if the workers wear special clothes, the special equipment they use, why they like their job, any particular problems they have, whether they make anything or provide a service to people, what sort of things are delivered both in and out of the workplace, if the workers are from the local neighbourhood or whether they travel from further away, what safety issues are involved. Take photographs, if possible. Ensure that the children are appreciative of the time given to them and express thanks to the person involved.

Recording

Suggest the children record the experience of their visit or meeting with the work person, in words and pictures.

Plenary

Recall highlights of the visit. Ask the children what qualities they think the worker in question has to have for the job. Perhaps they need to be extra friendly, particularly careful, good at drawing, keep very clean, and so on. If appropriate, consider why this particular job is important in the locality. For instance, it may be necessary for several people to have jobs at the local medical centre because there are many people living in the area, all of whom need to be able to seek help when they are ill.

6

Work and play

GEOGRAPHY

ACTIVITY 3

WHERE WORK IS DONE AROUND HERE

Learning objective
To develop an overall picture of where different types of work are carried out in the locality, by using a map with a key.

Resources
A specially made large-scale map of the neighbourhood (perhaps use the map from previous activities with which the children are by now familiar; it might be a good idea to make a new copy of this map for this particular activity); coloured stickers; felt-tipped pens.

Preparation
Look at the types of work done in the immediate area and decide how best to present the information on a map. Try to find categories which represent the types of work characteristic of the area. Perhaps a number of people find work in shops and cafés. Perhaps there are factories and warehouses nearby. The area might be mainly rural, in which case farming could be an important occupation. According to what needs to be shown on the map, draw simple symbols on coloured stickers, for example yellow for shops, green for farms, orange for schools and so on. Provide a special category for people who are doing their jobs in the streets – police, crossing patrols, postal workers.

Activity
Referring to the previous activities, ask the children to remind each other of what type of work is done by people in the area around the school. Explain that it would be useful to make a plan showing the workplaces. Show the children a simple plan of the locality and ask them to suggest the buildings which should be represented – perhaps shops, a factory, warehouse, garage and so on. Explain how useful a colour-coding system can be, and show the children the stickers to be used. The children can take it in turns to select the most suitable sticker to match to a workplace on the map.

  If there are open spaces or the area is more rural, encourage the children to decide what the land itself is used for. Perhaps there is farming, a park or lake. Consider the people who work in these places. Use stickers again to represent the working areas on the map.

  Show the children how to use one of each of the coloured stickers to make a key which should be displayed next to the plan.

When the map has been completed, ask the children some questions which require them to make use of the key. For example, in which street will they find the most people working in shops? How can they find out where there is a garage where people are working? What do the purple stickers tell them?

Differentiation
Children:
■ are aware that a coloured sticker on a map represents a type of work done in the area
■ associate coloured stickers with a key and can explain how to use a map which shows where different areas of work are carried out
■ use a map to make an assessment of the type of work available in the locality and where it takes place.

Plenary

Talk about the main type of work in the area and which type of buildings provide the most work. Is this work centred in one special area of the neighbourhood? What sort of work is limited? Point out that for people living in other areas there could be quite different jobs available in their locality.

Display

Give the map a title, perhaps 'Where people work around here', and display it with the work from the two previous activities.

GEOGRAPHY

ACTIVITY 4

WHERE DO YOU GO TO PLAY?

Learning objective

To identify suitable and safe playing areas and leisure facilities in the neighbourhood and understand the need for such facilities locally.

Resources

Photographs or video film of children enjoying themselves; simple large-scale map and aerial photograph of the area; leaflets about local familiar places; paper; pencils and crayons.

Preparation

Find out about local leisure facilities; collect advertisements from local newspapers and community magazines which describe leisure opportunities; display newspaper pictures and photographs of local events and activities.

Activity

With the children, talk about leaving their house and going somewhere nearby to play or enjoy themselves. Where do their parents or older siblings take them? Perhaps there is a park or sports field in the area. Locate these places on a large-scale map and look at an aerial photograph of the neighbourhood to see if these green areas are visible.

Discuss what the children like to do when they get there. Do they walk, play on the swings and so on, ride bikes, skateboard? Are there footpaths for walking in the locality, somewhere to exercise a dog? Consider whether these outdoor places are safe for young children. What dangers might there be? Would the children be able to spot an unsafe or unsuitable piece of equipment or another dangerous situation? Emphasise the need for a known adult to accompany the children. Show photographs or video film of children playing, to promote discussion. Do the children think they are fortunate in having a variety of safe play areas close to their homes or are they limited in what they can do?

Move on to talking about indoor leisure opportunities available locally. Perhaps there is a sports centre with a swimming pool. Is there a library or museum the children could visit? Find out if any of the children belong to clubs which operate locally – perhaps a sports club, church club or a club where they go to learn something new such as dancing or model making. Do the children know of clubs that older children can go to?

6

Work and play

Discuss the advantages of going out to nearby places for leisure activities – they are easy to reach on foot and you don't waste time getting there, for example. Talk about getting to know other people in the community and making new friends.

Recording
Ask the children to record where they like to go and play. They should draw their favourite place in the area for enjoying themselves and write words or sentences explaining some of the things they do there. Encourage some children to consider all the local amenities and comment on the range available for them.

Differentiation
Children:
■ are aware of local amenities and record with drawings and words what they like to do
■ know about a range of local amenities and record with drawings and sentences what they like to do
■ comment on the range of local opportunities for children's play in the area and record what they like to do.

Plenary
Ask the children why they think we need a range of places nearby for leisure facilities. Would they get bored without extra things to do? Perhaps they can find out new things, new interests, meet friends and get exercise. Does their neighbourhood supply their needs? Can everyone find something to their liking to do?

Display
Mark on the map the places the children have talked about. Use a key which the children should now be familiar with using. Indicate where the same places are on an aerial photograph. Display the photographs of children playing.

GEOGRAPHY

ACTIVITY 5

HOW DO YOU ENJOY YOURSELF?

Learning objective
To find out how adults like to spend their leisure time in the local area by conducting a survey.

Resources
Leaflets, newspaper advertisements, local magazines, large-scale map and aerial photograph of the area (as used in the previous activity); large sheet of paper for making preliminary list; felt-tipped pens.

Preparation
Find out what leisure facilities are available for adults in the locality and then decide what form the survey will take. Depending on the facilities available, be prepared to guide the children towards devising the survey so that the results will be useful. Will you include both indoor and outdoor opportunities? Will the activities be just those connected with sport and exercise? Will pubs and libraries be included? What about clubs in the area people might go to? Are there church-connected activities the children might want to talk about? Will the

questions simply require a yes or no answer? Perhaps the terms *sometimes*, *often* and *never* might be appropriate. Do not plan for too many questions, and perhaps leave space for adults to comment on facilities they would use but are not available. Be prepared to group activities into broad bands if there are lots of suggestions, or split categories if choice is limited. Decide who the children will ask, perhaps two people at home. Consider whether an accompanying letter is needed so that parents and carers will understand what the children are doing.

Plan when the introductory session will take place, when the survey will be ready to go out to parents and when to expect the results back. Allow time for reading the results and making conclusions.

Activity

Ask the children to help you make a list of all the places in the neighbourhood where adults can spend their leisure time. During the discussion refer to the large-scale map and aerial photograph so that the children are clear about which places they mean. Comment on whether there are plenty of places or whether it is difficult to think of any suitable venues.

Then ask the children how they could find out whether the adults in the area use any of these facilities. They will suggest asking parents and relations. Ask what would be a good way of doing this so that the children would not forget and everyone can look at the results. Talk about conducting a survey. Guide the children towards an ideal format, explaining that the questions must be easy to understand and the answers easy to interpret. When all decisions have been made, explain that the survey needs to be printed out so that the children can take one or two home to get the answers. Talk about asking one or two adults at home.

If appropriate, allow some children to help with the typing and printing of the survey. When it is ready, show it to everyone and read through the questions. Suggest the children might like to read the questions to the adults and fill in the answers themselves when at home. Tell the children when you would like to have the answers back at school.

After a suitable interval, look at the survey sheets with the children. Talk about how to get the information you want from the answers. Suggest pairs of children collate different parts of the survey, counting similar answers and recording the results.

Look at the findings and, if appropriate, make a graph. The children can use the computer to print out the information they have discovered, for example *14 people use the leisure centre; 3 people play cricket.*

Differentiation

Children:
- make suggestions for a survey and help with collating results
- help to devise a survey, and collate some of the results
- provide useful ideas for devising a survey, collate results with the help of a graph and draw conclusions.

Plenary

Ask what is the most popular leisure activity of adults in the area. Are the children surprised or is it what they expected? Do the children think the local facilities are well used? If not, is it because people go elsewhere? Are they not interested in what is available? Why is it a good thing if people use what is available locally? Emphasise the sense of community which develops when people meet each other often, and the importance of supporting local facilities, especially as many people can find work there.

Display

Display the information gleaned from the survey so that adults who have participated as well as the children can see the results.

The job I would like

What would you like to do?

_____

_____

Where would you work?

_____

_____

What would you use in your job?

_____

_____

Would you wear special clothes?

_____

_____

Draw a picture of yourself doing this job.

Display

It is important to display as much of the children's work as is possible. Making their efforts available for others to see not only adds value and prestige to what the children have achieved but also emphasises the importance of the information they have collected and the investigations they have made about their neighbourhood.

If children know that their work will be valued and available for others to see, they will take more care over presentation. At this stage of their development, the habit of always producing their best efforts can be encouraged.

Individual presentation

Collect each child's individual work – drawings, completed worksheets, written pieces and so on – and present them in a folder or as a booklet which they can personalise and show to each other and parents.

Provide photocopies to add to the children's collection of work, of photographs or pictures of local buildings and other neighbourhood features for the children to include alongside their own work.

Classroom display

Start to build up a display as soon as the work on *Around our school* begins. The displays will evolve over the weeks as the work progresses.

It can be useful to display each child's work relating to any specific activity, in a temporary way, perhaps with Blu-Tack, so that discussion and evaluation can take place and the work can be admired. Make sure the work is at a level where it can be easily seen by the children.

Where appropriate, photocopy and enlarge some parts of individuals' work to use with a display.

If space is limited in the classroom, extend the display into the corridor or hall.

The children's work and resources from the different sections of this topic can make separate but linked displays. If space allows, display each theme of each section around the classroom and other areas of the school. Try to give each theme an individual characteristic, using different display techniques such as colour scheme, arrangement of material, a border, emphasis of the printed word and so on.

Frequently refer to the displays, using them as the topic progresses and evolves, reminding the children how different elements of their work are linked.

Suggestions for display for each section
What can we see from our school?
■ Begin by making a temporary display by attaching each child's work from activity 1 to the wall while the features are discussed. Photocopy any drawings to be used later in the permanent display.
■ Use the patterns created from the children's observations to make a frieze or border for the display; include as part of the display, photographs of the features from which the patterns evolved.
■ As the other activities proceed, add to the display the aerial photograph showing the school and surrounding area, drawings and explanations of near and far features from the children's work together with any photographs available, drawings and other pictures of the church, and examples of the children's work relating to what passes by the school. Use the

signpost pointers as features and perhaps add the words *north, south, east* and *west* to remind the children of the directions in which things were seen. Add appropriate key words and headings, such as *nearby, far away, the church*, and names of specific local features which have been discussed during the activities for this section.

Where do I live?
■ Make a temporary display to begin with of the children's pictures of their houses.
■ Use the rubbings as a background and border as well as making some an important feature of the display.
■ Display the children's house pictures, each with an envelope giving their address.
■ Display the large-scale map with the stickers showing the locations of the children's homes, perhaps with lengths of coloured wool or string connecting house picture and address with location.
■ Display the graph which shows how children travel to school and use it in discussion.
■ Use any remaining space to include pictures and photographs of different types of houses with suitable headings.
■ Make available the children's maps of their routes home, perhaps in a folder or box nearby.

Buildings and features round and about
■ Build up a montage of the buildings and features of the neighbourhood, using children's drawings and other pictures and photographs.
■ Emphasise the importance of landmarks, both local and further afield, within a special part of the display, explaining their significance. Include the map showing local landmarks.
■ Display the chart of symbols representing buildings.
■ Display the children's rug/fabric designs, if possible enlarging or reproducing some of them to use as a border or background.
■ The 'work of art' will need a prominent safe position and should be the focal point of this section.

Visiting a church
■ If the church is the subject of the 'work of art', make this the eventual focal point of this display.
■ Reproduce the children's impressions from their church visit in large lettering and arrange them around any work about the church.
■ Display the children's observational drawings with explanations as to where and how they were carried out.
■ Use relevant printed material about the church, postcards, booklets and models as well as Christian artefacts and add it to the information gained from the visit.

What is it like around here?
■ Build up a montage of photographs and children's work to give an impression of the local area.
■ Include street scenes, busy and quiet areas, 'nice' places and 'nasty' spots, changes occurring. Unattractive areas cannot be ignored but emphasise the positive aspects of the local environment.
■ Display the map for visitors prominently, perhaps in the entrance hall or other communal area of the school.

Work and play
■ Divide a display board diagonally or vertically to make a distinction between work and play.
■ Display the two lists of jobs with their photographs in the work section along the map of workplaces.
■ In the leisure section, display the photographs and children's work showing the range of leisure facilities.
■ Display an explanation, the results and conclusions of the survey.

Assessment

At the end of the topic *Around our school*:

GEOGRAPHY

■ Are the children more aware of what happens in their locality and talk confidently about their neighbourhood?
■ Can they orientate themselves in relation to their school, home, surrounding features and places further afield?
■ Are they familiar with local work and leisure facilities?
■ Are they aware of the influence of human activity upon their neighbourhood, and do they know that people play a part in shaping the environment?
■ Can they interpret a large-scale map of their area, knowing that it represents a range of features and understand the importance of a key?
■ Have they developed an increased geographical vocabulary?
■ Can they make relevant comments and give opinions on their neighbourhood?
■ Are they able to collect information away from the classroom?

ART & DESIGN

■ Can the children attempt observational drawings?
■ Can they explore ideas in shape and pattern?
■ Are they able to use a range of tools and techniques?
■ Can they collaborate to create a work of art?

RE

■ Do the children understand that a Christian church is a special place for those who worship there?
■ Can they recognise Christian artefacts and begin to understand something of their significance?

Drawing the topic to a close

Plan a special event to mark the end of this project so that the children can demonstrate the extent of their investigations and artwork and show to a wider audience the information they have collected about their locality. A special event will show the children that their work is respected and valued and useful not only to themselves but to adults and other children. Parents can see what their children have been involved with over the weeks.

Invite other classes, parents and other visitors into the classroom to see an exhibition of the work. Encourage the children to give the adults they know a guided tour of the displays in the classroom, offering explanations and answering questions. Set aside a part of a day or evening to coincide with a parents' meeting or sports event at the school. Also encourage parents to drop in at other convenient times.

Arrange a special assembly centred on an area of the work the children have been particularly enthusiastic about. This can be performed for the rest of the school or at an informal gathering of parents, perhaps in the classroom where the displays can be admired.

It might be appropriate to exhibit the children's work in the community for an even wider audience. There might be a vacant shop window, a display board in the library or community centre where the work can be displayed.